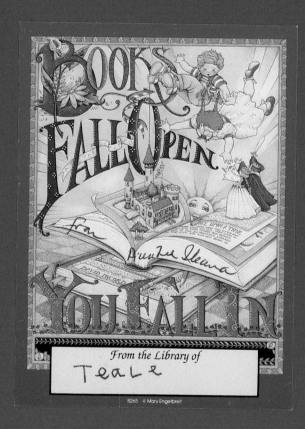

BOOKS FALL OPEN
YOU FALL IN

ONCE UPON A TIME

Fran

Aunte Ilcana

DAVID MCCORD

From the Library of

TeaLe

B265 © Mary Engelbreit

TAOS PUEBLO
Painted Stories

Jonathan Warm Day

Taos Pueblo 2005

TAOS PUEBLO
Painted Stories

Jonathan Warm Day

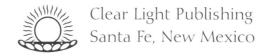
Clear Light Publishing
Santa Fe, New Mexico

©2004 Jonathan Warm Day
Clear Light Publishing
823 Don Diego
Santa Fe, New Mexico 87505
www.clearlightbooks.com

First Edition
10 9 8 7 6 5 4 3 2 1

Library of Congress Cataloging-in-Publication Data

Warm Day, Jonathan.
  Taos Pueblo : painted stories / by Jonathan Warm Day.— 1st ed.
      p. cm.
  ISBN 1-57416-080-X (hardcover)
  1. Taos Indians — Social life and customs. 2. Taos art. 3. Indian painting — New Mexico — Taos Pueblo. 4. Taos Pueblo (N.M.) — Social life and customs. I. Title.
  E99.T2W37 2004
  978.9004'97496 — dc22

                                                                                        2003027231

All illustrations ©Jonathan Warm Day
Art Photography ©Venus Masci & Phil Kagan
Cover Art: *The Time It Snowed*, acrylic on canvas, 16" x 40"
Cover design by Jonathan Warm Day

Printed in Korea

CONTENTS

Fall

Winter

Paintings in This Book

Special Thanks

Foreword

With each passing season, memories and traditions are being lost, as indigenous people struggle to embrace their identity while trying to cope with their ever-changing surroundings. I was raised in Taos Pueblo, New Mexico, with the knowledge of its sometimes tragic history. Today the villagers work and play where battles have been fought for survival. As a parent, I find personal conflict with the changing times, and I am trying to help to find a balance between the old and the new for my own daughters and their generation.

Every generation has had and will have its own issues, so I believe that in this beautiful and sometimes confusing life, each of us must be given the opportunity to express ourself wisely, without prejudice. Only then can we live in harmony with our surroundings.

Putting this book together has been a labor of love, but it also has come with some apprehension at times because of our tribe's nature, which discourages documenting our religion and history. Our ancestors chose secrecy, because others wanted to condemn and destroy what they couldn't understand.

In my work, I have tried to capture those moments that I believe existed in this valley between those harsh and challenging times and the present. I wish that I could have somehow also captured the sounds of laughter and the smells of all the traditional foods or the feelings of different emotions, like how one feels when watching the bright, velvet-like sunsets at the end of each full day.

I feel fortunate enough to have witnessed some of the old customs—like the piles of hay in the corrals and the family cornhusking get-togethers in autumn. My mouth still waters when I think of the wild pigeons that we hunted as youths and my grandmother cooked in her micaceous clay pot. In committing these words and images to print, I hope to help preserve a record of the traditional life of our people and to educate those who know little of us, desiring that increased knowledge and understanding will help all of us to live better with one another and with the natural world.

Jonathan Warm Day

SPRING

The chattering sound of "ick, ick, ick" echoed through the chilly morning air, but the lone flicker perched high atop the bare cottonwood tree was kept hidden from the many Pueblo eyes. The people were eagerly searching for one of the traditional messengers of spring.

Taos Pueblo

High above Taos Pueblo, a clean sparkling river flowed from the sacred Blue Lake, hidden among the tree-covered mountains. It wound its way down to the village, spreading across the valley through ancient ditches and watering the crops. It flowed past thick forests of aspen, spruce and other trees, which the Natives used for making roofs for their homes and fences for their corrals.

The mountains themselves were home to many kinds of wild animals that the Natives hunted for food and clothing. From tanned deer and elk skins, they sewed moccasins and leggings. They also made hand-made drums that echoed within the old adobe walls during village celebrations dating back to ancient times. Some of these were dances to honor the animals for their gifts to the people.

A Red Willow Place

*t*oday the Taos people still live in this beautiful valley. While being surrounded by an ever-changing world and having to adopt some of the habits of outsiders, they are trying to hold onto their traditions as well. They still live in their ancient village, which looks much the same as it did when the early Spanish explorers arrived. Their main source of surface water is still the stream that has always flowed through the center of the village from their sacred Blue Lake. They still speak their ancient unwritten language called Tiwa, used by only a few other related tribes. They choose to refer to themselves as the people living in "a red willow place."

Water Birds

Today, when the elders speak of the past, the village children can relate to their stories, because Taos Pueblo has changed very little. This is especially true during the celebrations that have been passed down from generation to generation. At certain moments, it seems that time stands still.

And as happened in the old days, the Natives share the Earth with the natural world. For example, they are often accompanied to the fresh-water stream by water birds, or swallows.

Captured in Clay

Scattered throughout the valley and beyond are many abandoned ruins. These were left behind by the ancestors of the present-day tribes, still living strong along the Big River (Río Grande).

One of the most important talents the Ancient Ones left behind is the ability to mold clay into beautiful yet useful art. Some pots, utensils and small clay figures have survived for thousands of years.

Each artist had his or her own spiritual relationship with Mother Earth, from which the clay was dug. Today many Native artists still practice and teach this art to new generations, using the same centuries-old techniques. Today's young artists are learning how to have their visions captured in clay.

Prized Possessions

During most celebrations, the women proudly carried food in their prized possessions—intricately decorated yet useful clay pots. Some were made by other tribes and some were their own creations, formed from the shiny micaceous clay dug from the sides of the nearby arroyos and washes. Equally useful and beautiful were the baskets made of tightly woven grass and other plant fibers. These usually came from the neighboring Apache tribes.

The Drum Maker

The village always seemed to be preparing for ceremonies or social feast days. These colorful and spiritual events were meant to help connect the people with the cycles of the seasons and nature's gifts. The echoes of the ceremonial drums sounded like the thunder that beat against the canyon walls, and the feet of the Corn Dancers touched the Earth like the rains that fell afterward.

The drum maker sought out dry aspen trees from the mountains or fallen cottonwood trees along the riverbanks. To make a drum, he would first hollow out a log's soft center. After the log was allowed to dry, the drum maker stretched damp, thick rawhide on one or both of its sides. He next would lace the log from top to bottom with damp strips of rawhide. When the drum was tied and completely dry, its beating would help announce joyous gatherings.

The Song of the Meadowlark

Some of the more lasting and memorable lessons of childhood were the ones learned from nature. In the spring, it was easy to see the love and devotion that animals and birds had for their young. After summer was over, one could feel melancholy while gazing at flocks of birds migrating across the autumn sky.

To this very day, if one listens closely, the song of the meadowlark can still be heard in the valley. This bird sings wherever someone is plowing the fertile earth to plant seed, as generations have done before. The chattering of a flicker in early spring can make one feel as if waking from a long winter slumber. These occasions remind us of how we are a part of the natural world.

Sunrise

In the Taos valley, the people grew to understand and respect the seasons and their changes. Some plants and animals slept during the cold winter months, while others patiently waited for the land to warm again. Finally, the last of winter disappeared back into the earth, giving birth and reawakening activity once more. This was the same cycle of seasons that the villagers followed.

They also moved in harmony with the sun as it made its way across the big Southwestern sky. By the time the first glow of sunrise appeared in the east over the tree-covered horizon, most of the villagers were already up. When it finally disappeared beyond the faraway stretch of mesas to the west, they could say that their day had been fulfilled.

SUMMER

Summer brought the brilliant sun that gave spirit to each day. It was a time when the children learned to dance in the village square. On hot days, they laughed as they bared their skin in the cold waters of the stream. In the evenings, families would go outside to feel the calm, cool beauty of the night.

The Village Criers

Their beckoning voices carrying far and wide from rooftops in the crisp morning air, the village criers paced back and forth, high atop their adobe stages. These men, dressed in traditional clothing and wrapped in their bright blankets, spoke with authority from tribal leaders. They delivered messages or called upon the people for different tasks, depending on the season. In the winter, it might be clearing the snow so that the people could move about easier. In the springtime, it might be cleaning of the ditches and mending of community fences. Throughout the year, the village criers would also summon the people to perform the ancient ceremonial dances.

Eagles Dancing

Dances have always been an important part of Pueblo life, partly because they gave the people a spiritual way to connect with the cycles of nature and to show their gratitude. The people also believed dancing helped bring success in hunting and farming.

Most of the Pueblo dances were intimate and ceremonial. They originated from within the tribe, and only tribal members performed them. As time went on, a few social dances began to appear. Some were introduced from other tribes, especially those of the Great Plains.

The people began learning the dances while still young children. In performing the Eagle Dance, for example, young boys became graceful eagles, soaring higher and higher in the sky. They danced to the elder's timelessly beautiful singing and drumming.

Day's Last Song

Just inside the main village walls are two Catholic churches. The older one is in ruins. It was destroyed centuries ago during an uprising against the American government by the Natives and their Spanish allies. With only its bell tower remaining, it is now used as a cemetery.

Sometime later, the villagers built the present St. Jerome Chapel a short distance away. The chapel's architecture has changed several times since its original construction.

Today, the bells of this small chapel still ring, inviting villagers and visitors alike through its doors. When the church commemorates its celebrations, the Taos people join in. They also perform their own ancient rituals. It is quite amazing to hear the day's last song above the ringing of the bells.

The Sun's Last Breath

The vast clear open sky of the Southwest has always provided breathtaking vistas. In the cool summer evenings, the villagers would sometimes climb up on their rooftops and gaze at the spectacular sunset, its colors both bright and soft as if painted on velvet. They watched as the sun's last breath blew across the horizon from far beyond the big river and mesas to the west.

Equally beautiful was how the winter landscape appeared at sunset. A soft pinkish blanket would cover the valley, just as everyone was preparing to retreat into their warm homes for the night.

Even today, villagers and visitors alike marvel at the sunsets, which often resemble a brightly colored trade blanket stretching across the western sky.

When the Moon Came Out

After a long day of work, the people of the village would look forward to going outdoors in the cool evenings. When the moon came out on crystal-clear, starry nights, some of the young men would meet on the middle footbridge. There they would stand together, singing and swaying in time to their music. Some songs had no words but beautiful melodies. Others had melancholy messages identifiable only by the Native people, while a few of the newer ones were love songs. The young men serenaded the villagers, with the stream trickling in harmony below.

The people of the village would find comfort and joy as they listened to the old and new songs that carried for long distances in the crisp night air. Even those who lived in their summer homesteads far beyond the ancient village walls were able to hear and enjoy them.

FALL

Autumn turned the Taos area into a pageant of color. High in the mountains, the aspens glittered a magical yellow, as they seemed to softly whisper to one another in the breeze. On the valley floor, patches of golden chamisa stood waiting, as if posing for admirers.

Scattered throughout the village were families shucking their piles of harvested corn. Laughing and reminiscing, they worked amid the rows of naked stalks. When the autumn breeze weaved about the fields, the brittle stalks sounded like the gourd rattles of approaching Corn Dancers.

Village Ponies

The earliest form of transportation for the Natives was the horse, introduced to them by the early European explorers. These big animals quickly adapted to the terrain, as did the Natives to the animals. The people immediately saw that they could use horses for traveling far and near as well as for heavy work, like plowing the fields or hauling heavy logs for home building.

As time passed, riders became younger and more skilled at handling horses. One of the greatest joys for the young boys was racing their fast village ponies with the wind in their faces. Both boys and girls liked taking tranquil autumn rides into the high colorful mountains.

Bountiful Harvest

The history of the Native people who settled in this valley is as colorful as their landscape. They have always been hunters, gatherers and farmers, living in harmony with their surroundings. After starting with small plots, they became seasoned growers of big fields of wheat and other crops. When their hard work and prayers yielded a bountiful harvest, they had much to be thankful for.

History showed that other tribes fled or were eventually displaced by non-Indian people who came to conquer and change them. The Taos people survived, however, because they could produce the food that the invaders needed.

The Village Gold

Autumn's arrival in the valley meant it was time to harvest both wild and planted crops. This was probably the busiest of all seasons. Surrounded by brilliant golden foliage, entire families spent their days shucking corn in the fields. Afterward, the rattling of horse-drawn wagons carrying mounds of harvested corn could be heard bouncing up and down the narrow paths. The days were still long and warm, and the villagers, especially the children, savored the sunlight for as long as possible.

When all the work was done, the families began careful preparation for the tribe's annual harvest celebration. At sunrise on that eventful day, the men of the village competed in a ceremonial footrace. Throughout the day, farmers and craftsmen from far and near showed and traded their wares and harvested goods. The day's activities eventually ended, when the ceremonial clowns magically appeared to entertain the waiting crowds.

Baskets of Piñon

In the fall, with lunches packed and ready for a full day's outing, the villagers would wander out into the crisp autumn morning in search of nature's special treats. Many were looking for nuts of the piñon pine— small tasty nuts that when ripe fall to the ground from their sticky cones. After picking all day, they would gradually make their way back to the village with baskets full of nuts.

The people and all other living things could sense the changing of the seasons. Signals of autumn appeared, from the brilliantly colored landscape to the small animals and birds scurrying about in search of food to store away for colder days. Both people and animals would welcome the winter season thankfully prepared.

The Chokecherry Harvest

When the branches of the chokecherry trees became heavy with small, dark, round fruit, the harvest would begin. Throughout the valley, mothers and daughters—and sometimes whole families—would wait patiently for this special time.

The feathered ones the people called chokecherry birds in their Native Tiwa language would announce the start of the harvest. These small, heavy-beaked birds would appear as if by magic. They gathered in little flocks, signaling by loud bursts of warbling the choicest areas—where the ripened fruit was most plentiful.

In addition to chokecherries, the villagers hastened to gather wild plums, berries and tasty mushrooms before the end of the short gathering season. With nature's offerings overflowing during this time, there was plenty for all.

High Above the Valley

High above the valley, many species of wildlife continue to flourish. The Native people have spiritual ties to all these creatures and to the area itself, which their ancestors chose to call home.

This is a place where freshwater Native trout swim in the cold mountain streams, while wild sheep graze on grassy alpine meadows alongside the mule deer and elk.

These mountains have always provided meat for physical nourishment of the villagers, but they also became a place for spiritual sanctuary and worship, at special sacred locations known only by the Taos people.

A Moment for All

The first Natives that settled in the valley were farmers and gatherers, much like the other tribes that came to the desert Southwest. However, as they moved into the shadows of the chain of mountains that stretched far to the north, they also became great hunters of big animals.

Whenever meat was needed, the men of the village would venture into the mountains to hunt deer, elk and wild sheep. Sometimes they went farther, over the mountain range to the grassy plains that sloped up the eastern side, where they hunted the giant buffalo.

These hunters never forgot their families depending on them or the dangers that they might encounter. They knew that skill alone wasn't enough, so they always spent time in prayer before and after each trip.

After a successful hunt, the entire village would hold colorful celebrations. Even today, Natives and visitors alike can still witness these ancient activities. The people still pay homage to those animals that give them life.

New Moccasins

When the ceremonial dancers touched the Earth with their feet, one reason they were dancing was to show their gratitude for nature's blessings. Nature was grand in many ways. It was the soft pale snowy landscape at sundown, so breathtakingly beautiful that one forgot the cold. It was the solitary knowledge gained by a young boy irrigating a cornfield. It was the melancholy one sensed while watching a distant flock of geese floating across the autumn sky. It was the taking of a life during a deer hunt to provide food for the family table and the new moccasins that touched the Earth once again in gratitude.

WINTER

After the last of the leaves fell to the ground, a white melancholy veil would settle upon the sacred mountain, announcing the beginning of a long winter. The final remaining villagers who tended to small summer homesteads beyond the ancient walls would come back inside to their warm adobe dwellings, to wait out the long winter ahead. There, the peaceful season of stories, good food and family togetherness would continue until the arrival of a new year.

The Wood Cutter

When the last of the autumn foliage gave way to the first dusting of snow, families would begin gathering in the evening around a warm glowing fireplace, eating hot food and enjoying the telling of old stories. Outside their adobe homes would be piles of dry wood, usually piñon or cedar, which would keep them comfortable until the ground gradually warmed again. The wood had been gathered from the surrounding foothills by the wood cutter and carried out upon the back of his trusted donkey.

The Scent of Cedar & Piñon

As evening fell upon everyone within the old village wall, the scent of cedar and piñon burning filled the cold night air. The people would be using the wood for light, warmth and baking, just as they had for generations. Even today, the scent of piñon smoke rising from a chimney or of cedar crackling inside an outdoor oven triggers a loving nostalgia. It makes one aware of the uniqueness of being able to live in both the traditional and modern worlds.

Oven-Baked Bread

*t*he aroma of fresh oven-baked bread and other traditional foods always filled the homes of the villagers during ceremonial events and other social gatherings. The meal preparation helped bring people together almost as much as the events themselves.

Great feast days, like the harvest celebrations, and ceremonial events, such as the Deer and Buffalo Dances, brought people from all around, including new friends as well as more distant family members. These and the more intimate gatherings helped carry on the village traditions, especially for the children, who would later continue them with their own families. The joyous gatherings would become memories retold to grandchildren.

A Night for Songs & Stories

During the long, cold winter nights, families would gather together around a warm, bright, crackling fireplace. They would spend the evening enjoying traditional foods and the songs and stories of the village elders.

The children would usually beg to hear stories about the clever coyote. The adventures featuring this trickster animal would have the children sitting up straight, wide-eyed, until the last word was spoken. Other stories included personal memories and true accounts of the tribe's history that the elders felt the young needed to eventually pass down.

The elders also told of marauding tribes that came to this valley long, long ago. More recent stories showed how their people eventually sought refuge among some of these same tribes, when new enemies came to conquer and try to change their way of life forever. Today families still gather for winter nights of songs and stories, reliving memories and passing down the ancient accounts that unite the people as a tribe.

Winter Rabbit Hunt

Because the springtime streams swollen from melted mountain snow and the summer rains kept the valley alive, farming has been a village tradition from the very beginning. During winter, even though the people could draw upon their stored food, they would sometimes like the addition of fresh meat.

During the cold months, like many other indigenous hunters, the Taos people would wander nearby for a winter rabbit hunt. Weather permitting, they would sometimes journey farther up into the mountains for several days of deer or elk hunting. When an animal was taken, the hunter never forgot to thank it with a prayer for having provided for his survival.

Watching the Deer Dancers

Watching the ancient pageantry of the Deer Dance was highly anticipated throughout the village. Even the audience was colorful, especially the women. They wore their traditional finery of long flowing dresses and shiny, brightly colored shawls with spiraling fringes. Everyone came together to honor the graceful deer and watch the dancers enact its life. The cycle of the seasons and traditions had again gone full circle, as it had for centuries.

Paintings in This Book

The following paintings by Jonathan Warm Day are reproduced in this book.

Baskets of Piñon, 36" x 36" (p. 32); *Bountiful Harvest*, 18" x 14" (p. 29); *Captured in Clay*, 30" x 36" (p. 7); *Chokecherry Harvest*, 45" x 45" (p. 35); *Day's Last Song*, 25" x 17" (p. 21); *Drum Maker*, 12" x 10" (p. 11); *Eagles Dancing*, 32" x 44" (p. 19); *High Above the Valley*, 25" x 34" (p. 37); *Moment for All*, 48" x 36" (p. 38); *New Moccasins*, 16" x 20" (p. 41); *Night for Song and Stories*, 38" x 50" (p. 49); *Oven Baked Bread*, 15" x 20" (p. 47); *Prized Possessions*, 29" x 54" (p. 9); *Red Willow Place*, 22" x 28" (p. 3); *Scent of Cedar & Piñon*, 22" x 30" (p. 45); *Song of the Meadow Lark*, 26" x 36" (p. 13); *Sun's Last Breath*, 14" x 18" (p. 23); *Sunrise*, 16" x 12" (p. 14); *Taos Pueblo*, 48" x 36" (p. viii); *Time It Snowed*, 16" x 40" (cover); *Village Crier*, 8" x 16" (p. 16); *Village Gold*, 36" x 48" (p. 30); *Village Ponies*, 22" x 28" (p. 26); *Watching the Deer Dancers*, 24" x 28" (p. 53); *Water Birds*, 48" x 36" (p. 4); *When the Moon Came Out*, 23" x 26" (p. 25); *Winter Rabbit Hunt*, 36" x 30" (p. 50); *Wood Cutter*, 36" x 48" (p. 42).

All the original acrylic-on-canvas paintings, including the cover art, are available as Giclée prints from the artist. For more information, please visit Jonathan Warm Day's Web site at www.taospueblo.com/artists/warmday.php or e-mail jonathanwarmday@yahoo.com.

Jonathan Warm Day and his two daughters, Carly (l.) and Jade (r.).

Photo: Venus Masci

Special Thanks

To my family and friends, who have supported and encouraged this dream from the beginning, I give my greatest thanks. To the following: Tony Reyna, Helen (Chaya) Victor, Millicent Rogers Museum, Debra Whaley, Steve Villalobos, John and Marcine Landon, Arlene and Larry Egan, Dr. Del Endres, Lumina Greenway, Taos Talking Picture Festival, Ed and Trudy Healy, Wiz and Kika Allred, Sebia Hawkins and Clear Light Publishers—I give a special thank you.